T0208064

THE THREEFOLD MINISTRY OF CHRIST

FROM THE EARTH INTO THE GRAVE

Louimaire Moléon Guillaume

Order this book online at www.trafford.com
or email orders@trafford.com

Most Trafford titles are also available at major online book retailers.

Printed in the United States of America.

ISBN: 978-1-4669-2240-2 (sc)
ISBN: 978-1-4669-2241-9 (e)

Trafford rev. 04/14/2012

 www.trafford.com

North America & international
toll-free: 1 888 232 4444 (USA & Canada)
phone: 250 383 6864 ♦ fax: 812 355 4082

Dedicated to

Rev. Pastor Reynold Lorrius and Mrs Junie Lorrius

TABLE OF CONTENTS

*   *   *   *

1: The earthly Ministry of Christ

2: The Ministry of Christ upon the cross

3: The Ministry of Christ into the grave

*   *   *   *

PROLOGUE

Eight hundreds years before his birth on the earth, the prophet Isaiah had discribed the Messiah who had to be born in Bethlehem, as a Child with a noble mission upon his shoulder to assume. To fulfill that mission with charisma and fairness, it had been given to Isaiah the prophet these five following titles to be borne by the Messiah: Isiaiah 9:5: For unto us a child is born, unto us a Son is given; and the government shall be upon his shoulder, and his name shall called Wonderful, Counsellor, the mighty God, the everlasting Father, the Prince of peace. There wasn't only the prophet Isiaiah who had received revelations on different names and titles for the holy Child. By the way, across all the Old Testament Bible, 366 prophecies have been found talking about his birth, his life, his Ministry, his treason, his arrest, his flagellation, his crucifixion, his death, his burial, his resurrection, his ascension to heaven and his second return to meet in the air, the triumphant Church, his Fiancé. 50 out of the 366 prophecies found in the Old Testament talk about the birth of Messiah. But, among all the ancient prophets who had received revelations on the holy Child, Isiaiah was the only one to be able to discribe Him with such precision and exactness. It is for the same reason that Isiaiah is called the messianic prophet. By the way, The names or the titles get their sacred value in the hebrew language. According to the jewish belief, in Israel, when a child is born, his parents don't haste to give him any kind type of name, because all his destiny will be for ever influenced by it. In fact, when a babe is born in Israel, very often, it is the jewish rabbi responsibility to pick names and to determine between them which one to be given to him. According to the jewish custom, when a child is born, usully, two different names are chosen for him; a public and a secret one. The hidden name is kept to be revealed until the evolution of this person shows that she deserves to be called so. Otherwise, the secret name might be never revealed. It is the reason why, in Israel, for the most part of the names given to people, they are chosen from the Bible. But, with regard to this passage from Isiaiah 9:5, instead of being proper names, it is more appropriate to talk about five different titles to be given to the holy Child. Be that as it may, about the Messiah, it was God himself who had revealed to Isiaiah the prophet the titles to be given to the Messiah. It was according to God will to be so, for each of these five titles has an appropriate meaning, bound to the fulfillment of his messianic mission on the earth. When the Child Jesus was born in manger in Bethlehem, the first people who had admired him, were Mary his mother, Joseph his adoptive father, the shepherds guarding sheeps in the fields . . . , the magi from the East bringing to him the golden, the frenkincense and myrrh. Because of his messiahship, even the presents brought to he holy Child by the magi, had each one a symbolic meaning. In fact, the golden is the symbol of his kingship, the frenkincence is the symbol of his suffering and the myrrh is the symbol of his embalming, his burial.

=CHAPTER ONE=

I: 5 different titles
for one fulfilled mission

Isiaiah 9:5

For unto us a child is born, unto us a son is given; and the government shall be upon his shoulder; and his name shall be called Wonderful, Counsellor, The mighty God, The everlasting Father, The Prince of peace.

A: He shall be called: <u>Wonderful</u>

By definition, wonderful means: What is worthy of admiration; what is amazing; what evokes astonishment; what is surprising.

If the name or the title given to a child can determine his personality, his destiny, what's about Jesus-Christ? How his title <u>Wonderful</u> amazed the people living around him, in his messianic fulfillment of his earthly mission?

The amazedness and the wonderment of Jesus Ministry didn't consist only in his actions, his behavior, but in his way of speaking also.

Let us see Jesus in his behavior, when He was among men on the earth. No one can't find any kind of proof to deny this truth: Jesus is the only sinless Man who had ever lived on the earth, from his mother womb to his return to heaven. I mean by that, Jesus is the only infallible Man who had lived among sinners, but who got never contamineted by sin. No one can deny this fact. You can believe it without doubt and you can repeat it fearless of nothing and no one. It was a truth in the past, it is a truth in the present time and this truth will be infallaible in its exactness for ever more. I believe with all my heart and I ask you to put faith in it as it is: Jesus is the first and the last sinless Man who was living on the earth. For, from this generation to the next, no one of us will be able to do like he did. Because of that, the title <u>Wonderful</u> fits very well to Jesus reputation as Messiah. There are more facts than that. The Messiah was really a blameless one. Because, Jesus was born without sin; He grew up among men without sin; He began his Ministry without sin; He fulfiled it without sin; He was crucified without sin; He died on the cross without sin; He went down into the grave without sin; He rose from the death without sin; He had been for forty days in Galilee after his resurrection, showing himself more than 13 times to more than 533 people, without sin. And He went back to heaven without sin. Only a man like Jesus could fulfill the messianic mission in the fulness of holiness, according to God the Father. Because of that, Jesus deserves more than to be called <u>Wonderful</u>. During his Ministry on the earth, Jesus fulfiled miracles and prodigies that no man could not do. To number some of them, He rose Lazarus from the grave, after four days; He changed water into wine; He walked on the sea; He made blinds see; He made lames walk; He cast out and healed some demons-possed. For all these reasons and so many more, the title <u>Wonderful</u> fits very well to the messianic mission of Jesus-Christ on the earth. There are so many things to say about the title <u>Wonderful</u> of the Messiah that the list should be too long if I had to continue. So, if the wonderment of the holy Child can hid an other one, what is about the counsels of his messiahship?

=CHAPTER TWO=

II: Christ, an Ambassador from heaven

B: He shall be called: <u>Counsellor</u>

By definition, a counsellor is a peacemaker between two or more people whose relationship was prohibited for some reason during a long or a short period of time. A counsellor is also a reconciler, a mediator, like an ambassador, between two countries whose diplomatic relations were prohibited for certain reasons, and in his quality of peacemaker, the counsellor tries his best to re-establish dialogue and agreement between them. In the proceedings of God the Father, the messiahship of the Son was to come from heaven, to pay the price of mankind sin by his blood, to etablish a new agreement, in order to satisfy the righteousness of the Lord. The love of God was the reason of his proceedings through

Jesus who deserves the title of Counsellor. For, when Adam sinned in Eden against God laws, the diplomatic relations which existed before, between the kingdom of heaven and the earth were up side down for four thousand years. Therefore, because of mankind sin, Satan had the dominion over all the descendants of Adam, from one generation to the next. During that long period of time, no man was found qualified or worthy to re-establish the agreement between the kingdom of the earth and the kingdom of heaven; Only Jesus was found qualified and worthy to reconciliate the two kingdoms, like a reprochless Counsellor between God the Father, and mankind. Since then, because of the messiahship of Jesus, the Counsellor between God and mankind, the righteousness of the Lord is satisfied and that allows us to get forgiveness from heaven. All that becomes possible because of the proceedings of Jesus. So, in his quality of Mediator to reconciliate mankind with God, the Messiah deserves more than to get the title of a <u>Counsellor</u>. Above all, the Bible is full of counsels from Jesus for whatever issue, no matter what the situations; whether it be in spiritual realm or material domain. In his proceedings as Counsellor, the Messiah came to teach man how to reconciliate with himself; because the biggest drama of existence is when somebody does'nt love himself; he came to teach man how to reconciliate with God;

he came to teach man how to reconciliate with his neighbor. Jesus didn't only preach people the way to live, he let them see that in his behevior; Jesus didn't only teach people how to become a good heavently citizen but he taught them too the way to be a good earthly citizen. Let us take some biblical examples where Jesus used to give counsels to people:

Matthew 7:13: Enter ye in at the strait gate for wide is the gate, and broad is the way, that leadeth in destruction, and many there be which go in thereat.

Matthew 5:29: And if any right eye offend thee, pluck it out, and cast it from thee for it is profitable for thee that one of thy members should perish, and not that thy whole body should be cast into hell.

Mattew 5:40-42: And if any man will sue thee at the law, and take away thy coat, let him have thy cloke also. And whosoever shall compel thee to go a mile, go with him twain. Give to him that asketh thee, and from him that would barrow of thee turn not thou away.

Matthew 6:19-20: Lay not up for yourselves treasures upon earth, where moth and rust doth corrupt, and where thieves break through and steal. But lay up for yourselves treasures in heaven, where neither moth nor rust doth corrupt, and thieves do not break through nor steal. All these passages are full of counsels from Jesus, the Messiah.

The Bible is full of examples that let us see that the title Counsellor fits very well to the messiahship of Jesus. Above all, in his proceedings as Messiah, the holy Child came to counsel man to reconciliate with himself; he came to counsel man to reconciliate with God the Father; he came to counsel man to reconciliate with his neighbor.

C: He shall be called: The mighty God

There is no doubt about that, Jesus was the incarnation of the Father in human form. Why He came in human form and not in human nature? What is the difference between these two concepts? Response: with a human form, Jesus could not sin; with a human nature, Jesus-Christ shoulb be a sinner like you and I. This is why, Joseph was only the adoptive father of the Messiah. In fact, in Luke 1:34-35, when the angel Gabriel came from heaven to meet Mary unto the city of Galilee named Nazareth to give her the good news, he said: Hail, thou that art highly favoured, the Lord is with thee; blessed art thou among women. And when she saw him, she troubled at his saying, and cast in her mind what manner of situation this should be. And the angel said unto her, fear not, Mary: for thou hast found favour with God. And behold, thou shalt conceive in thy womb, and bring forth a son, and shalt call his name Jesus. He shall be great, and shall be called <u>the Son of the Highest</u>; and the Lord God shall give unto him the throne of his father David: and he shall reign over the house of Jacob for ever; and of his kingdom there shall be no end: Luke 1:28-33. According to the Bible, we can realize that the seed to conceive Jesus was not from a man, but from God himself. This is why Jesus did not take a human nature, but a human form. Because of that, He could not sin; He had the same divine nature than his Father. It's for the same reason that Jesus said in John 10:30: I and my Father are one.

D: He shall be called: <u>The everslasting</u> <u>Father</u>.

One of the most important part of the Bible concept that people have a certain doubt about, is to understand how God the Father can be equal to his Son Jesus—Christ. Eventhough the Bible is clear about that but, they are still confused to understand the way it works. I gonna try to make it clear for you. But, before I start, let me ask you a question: Why do you think that God the Father left the splendor of heaven to come down to our level like a Son? May the Holy Spirit help you to understand the answer that I am about to give you. Here is the first part of the answer: When Jesus says in John10:30: I and my Father are one, it's exactly what it is. To be understood better, Jesus said again, in an other passage, John 14:10: Believest thou not that I am in the Father, and the Father is in me? The works that I speak unto you I speak not of myself; but the Father that dwelleth in me, he doeth the works. Now, let me answer the question by explaining to you the reason why God the Father left the splendor of heaven to come down here as a Son. I don't even need to ask you an other question about that. Because, it is very obvious to you that you can't call somebody <<father>> if he has no son. It was the same thing for the Lord. When someone has no son, to avoid to call him <<father>>, you just call him by his ordinary name. The same rule is applied for a female. Don't you ever call a person of female sex either<<mother>> if she has no children. Because that does'nt make sense to her and to anybody around her. To understand me better, I'm gonna ask a question to you who are reading this book. Be ready to answer this question: Whether it be you are a man or a woman. If you don't have children and then, somebody calls you <<father or mother>>, tell me how you feel about that. Do you proud of it? If you don't have children, just because somebody calls so, do you fell like one? Absolutly not! It was exactly the same thing about God. At a certain period of time, no man on the earth could'nt call God <<Father>> because the idea of <<son>> wasn't conceived yet, to let men know about the sonship of God. Meanwhile, the only kind relationship which existed about man and God used to be between a Creator and his creatures. I mean, by that time, man could'nt call God <<father>>. To change this kind relationship between him and man, God took the resolution to send Jesus-Christ to become the <u>Son,</u> to be the bridge between him and man. It took God four thousands years before he revealed the Son to mankind; God had etablished a period of time to be accomplished before he sent the Son. This is exactly what we read in Galatians 4:4-5: But when the fulness of time has come, God sent forth his Son, made of a woman, made under the law, to redeem them that where under the law, that we might receive the adption of sons. Don't you ever forget what we are talking about now. I am about to explain to you the right way for someone to become the son of God. I want to let you understand that outside a relationship with Jesus, no one can be called <u>son of God</u>. The

Bible gets the evidence that Jesus is the only bridge between God and men. In return, outside of a relationship with Jesus, one can remain only a creature of God. Now, Let us go back to Galatians 4:4-5 to underline some very important words. Let us underline this phrase: <u>When the fulness of time has come.</u> Why do I ask you to underline it? The reason for that is just because I want you to pay attention to the fact that God was waiting for four thousands years before he sent his Son to redeem men from the curse of law. Why did God wait for so long before he sent Jesus? It's just becaue when God gave the authority to Adam to rule over the creation, the Creator shared his power with man, to take responsibility in leading the earthly affairs, with rectitude and fairness. After sharing his power and his authority with Adam to rule over the creation, God took a certain distance from ruling in man place. But, God knew the fulness of time given to man rulership: Four thousands years had to be fulfilled before that. We can call that a <u>time of probation</u>. There is an other expression that I want you to underline in the same chapter of Galatians 4:4-5: <u>Under the law.</u> Why God put men under the law, after Adam sinned against him? The reason is sample. A law becomes effective, only when you desobey this law. Otherwise, this law might remain effectless. But, when you do something wrong, immediately, you create the effectiveness of this law against yourself. It was what hapenned to Adam and was the reason why that put God men under the law for Adam sake; I mean, by desobeying the law, Adam created the effectiveness of the law. That means again, because the rebellion of Adam, God put all the human race on probation, giving to us the same law as a pedagogue to lead us, until he sent his Son Jesus to redeem men from the curse of the law. The last phrase I want you to underline is: <u>That we might receive the adoption of sons</u>. This is the most important part of the New Testament Bible to explain the relationship between God and men. This sonship is possible only through Jesus-Christ. If you pay attention to the same passage, the Bible makes it clear to our understanding, in saying: <u>We receive the adoption of sons.</u> There is a condition to become son of God. The condition is sample. If the Son is the only bridge between God and men, that means, to be connected with the father, we must be on Jesus expense. So, it's only when you pass by Jesus-Christ, you can become son of God. Because, no one can be born son of God; one can only become it. If you are on Jesus expense; you are on God expense; if you reject the Son, you reject the father. Let us see what the Bible says in John 5:22-23: For the father judgeth no man, but hath commited all judgment unto the Son. That all men should honour the Son as they honour the father. He that honoureth not the Son honoureth not the father which hath sent him. So, it's only through Jesus the relationship is effective and possible between God and men. The Bible has the evidence of that, let us read: John 1:12: But, as many as received him, to them gave the power to become the sons of God, even to them that believe on his name. So, you, who are reading this book, I invite you to be on Jesus expense if you want to be connected with God. Right now, you can call upon the name Jesus to be saved. I guarantee you, if you do that with all your heart, you'l be never a loser. Don't wait to understand God before you believe in God; don't you ever put in your mind that you're gonna understand this fathom mystery. For, the day you understand God, you become God. Believe first and after all, you will discover, little by little, the fathomeless of God love, not to become like him,

But you gonna get the evidence that the Son is equal to his Father because they have and they are the same divine nature. Let me say it an other way, in order to reach and to save men, it was God the Father himself who became the Son. This is exactly what Jesus try to explain to each and every one of us, in John 14:10 when he says: Believest thou not that I am in the Father, and the Father in me? The works that I speak unto you I speak not of myself; but the Father dwelleth in me, he doeth the works. So, when the prophet Isiaiah was told by God to call the Messiah: The everslasting Father, that simply means, it was the Father who came in human form to be born in a virgin to become flesh among us and like us. Why God became a man? Did you ever ask yourself this question? This is the most important thing to know about the messiahship of Christ. Let me try to give you a short answer. Here is it: God became a man, because the dominion over the creation was given to a man. This man was Adam: Genesis 1:27-28. When Adam failed, a man failed. So, if a man failed, a man had to come to save man from his failure. God made no mistake, because He sent the right person for the right mission: a sinless Man. If God had sent an angel to fulfill this kind mission, it should had been a mistake. Because the angels don't even understand the the depth of men salvation. Read 1Peter 1:12: This is what I call the concept of God who becomes man by the the incarnation. So, in the divine incarnation there is also the divine aquation: The Father+the Son=1: John 10:30: I and my Father are one. It is the same thing about the Trinity concept. The Bible can explain it to you. In the same aquation, God=Spirit; Spirit=God: Jean 4:24: God is a Spirit; and they that worship him must worship him in spirit and in truth.

E: He shall be called: <u>The Prince of peace.</u>

Before we start that, let me ask some questions. 1: Why did Isiaiah call the Messiah a Prince? Response 1: Isiaiah did not choose to call him a Prince, it was according to God will he gave this title to him. The Messiah is called <<Prince>> because his father, God, is the King of kings. 2: Why his father, God, is the King of kings? Response 2: His father, God, is the King of kings because he reigns over all the heavenly kingdom and then he has the authority on all the powers on the earth. 3: What kind of peace did the Messiah bring to deserve the title: <u>The Prince of peace?</u> Response 3: After the fall of Adam in Eden, because of his sin, the relationship between the kingdom of heaven and the earth was up side down. By disobedience against the divine authority, there was no peace between men and God; there was no peace between men and men and there was no individual peace eather. The situation was so confused that God was looking for Ambassador to re-establish the agreement between the two kingdoms. Only Jesus-Christ, the begottenson was qualified for this holy mission. It was the reason of his proceedings on the earth. When Jesus came, in his quality of Prince of peace, he brought three kinds of agreements on the earth:

a) The Prince of peace came to put men in agreement with God; because, without the peace of God, men are in trouble.

b) The Prince of peace came to put man in agreement with himself. Because, when somebody is in trouble with God, he can consider himself as his own enemy. It is the reason why very often one can commit suicide; it's just because a lack of peace in the heart creates around him a fathom hoplessness and sadness. But, when he receives from Jesus the peace of God, he feels free and his face is beamed of joy. Now, God puts in my heart to talk to you directly. I am talking to you who are reading this book, right now. I don't know what kind situation you are facing in your private life. Who knows? Maybe you are facing a problem that you can't talk about to no one; it might be somebody who raped you when you were a teenager; you are trying to keep that secret but that becomes day after day a burden on your heart. Sometimes, you feel so guilty that you want to commit suicide. Please, I beg you in the name of Jesus, don't commit suicide. Because, you have someone to confess your sins. God is waiting for you at any time; he wants to forgive your sins and write your name in the book of life. I know what I am talking about. There is some sin so hateful in someone life that there nothing to do to get rid of it, is to forgive the offenser. Otherwise, you will be wretch until you die. I can tell you the history of a woman who was raped in her very young age. It was so shameful that she decided to keep it secret. One day, she attended to an evangelical crusade. After the sermon, the pastor was told by God to invite first, all those who were sexually abused to come forward. A very old woman of 80 years came up and testified that she was raped by someone at 15. She was crying when she said it was for the first time she revealed that. She said again for 65 years she kept that secret, her heart was a real jail to lock-up people by resentment. After her testimony a crowd of people went to confess their sin for being abused the same way. If you are discribe by that or your case different, Jesus invites you to come put down your burden in saying: Matthew 11:28: Come unto me all ye that labour and are heavy laden, I will give you rest. After receiving the salvation and the forgiveness of your sins, whatever people did wrong to you, forgive them too, and feel free now to enjoy your journey. When you forgive your offensers, you live in peace with God, with yourself and your neighbour.

c) The Prince brought peace, to put men in agreement with men. This kind peace brought by the Prince-Messiah, is not like the world one. The kind peace that the Prince-Messiah gives is a lasting one: John 14:27: Peace I leave with you; my peace I give unto you: not as the world giveth, give I unto you. Let not your heart be troubled neither let it be afraid. Don't let this moment pass you by to surrender your life to Jesus, because God has a plan of salvation and forgiveness for you while Satan gets a hatefulness and a resentment one.

=CHAPTER THREE=

III: The plenitude of a successful Ministry

F): <u>The earthly Ministry of Christ</u>

According to the Bible, the Ministry of Christ on the earth, began just after his forty days and forty nights of fastings. (Matthew4:1-11); Matthew 4:12-25. Before the inauguration of Christ Ministry on the earth, he was submited by the Holy Ghost for a threefold temptation by the devil whose goal was to prevent him from doing according to his father will. Satan tried in three different occasions to seduce Jesus in his threefold dimension. Let me explain you how. In Matthew 4:3-4: when the tempter came to him, he said, if thou be the son of God, command that thes stones be made bread. But he answered and said. It is written, man shall not live by bread alone, but by every word that proceedeth out the mouth of God. In the first temptation, Satan tried to seduce Jesus in his body. For Satan knew that after his forty days and forty nights of fastings, Jesus was hungred. The other reason why the devil tried to seduce Jesus that way, was just because the Messiah came as a second Adam to release the challenge of the first one who failed in a forbidden fruit in Eden. Because he failed the first Adam in food, Satan thought that it should be an easy way to get seduced the second one. But the second Adam rebuked him by written words. Satan is not a naïve being in his way to attak people. The main goal of Satan attaks is always to subduce every human being in his threefold dimension. It was the same stratagem that he used to fail Jesus. The tempter failed in his first attak , by trying to seduce Jesus. In Matthew 4:5-7, the tempter came again and said to him: if thou be the son of God, cast thyself down for it is written. He shall give the angels charges concerning thee and in their hands they shall bear thee up last at any time thou dash thy foot against a stone. Jesus said unto him, it is written again the shall not tempt the Lord thy God. In the first temptation, Satan tried to seduce Jesus in his body. But, in the second temptation, it was in his soul that Satan tried to seduce Jesus. Why I say so? Let me explain you why and how the tempter processed to seduce Jesus in his soul by the second attempt. When the devil said to Jesus: if thou be the son of God, cast thyself down for it is written . . . , Jesus was tempted in his soul, for Satan knew that the soul is the center of the emotions of man. So, every time that someone hastes to act, according to his feelings, just to show off, without any ponderation, he becomes an easy prey to give way to the temptation. So, it is very easy to understand when people try to push you acting by emotions. Very often, you might be asked to release a challenge just in order to show off. This is why, in two occasions, Satan used the same little phrase: <u>if thou be the son of God</u> . . . If Jesus was an emotive person, that exciting little phrase only should be enough to drive him to do the show-off. But, the devil was rebuked again by written words. Therefore, it is a good example and a good lesson to be followed by any one of us whose emotions are skin-deep. You have no reason to let your feelings master you. Whatever the situation, take controle, take heed and don't loose your temper, for if you haste to act without any ponderation, in your coolness, you gonna be regret it. In regard of the Ministry of Christ upon the earth, there are so many authors who speak of it, that I think it willn't be a bad idea if I set aside some details to deal with the hard part. The Ministry upon the earth of Christ began in Capernaum to finish in Jerusalem at Golgotha. Betrayed by his own disciple

Judas, arrested by the roman soldiers, Jesus was forced to carry his cross to be crucified at Calvary. However, just after Jesus hanged up the cross, the second part of his Ministry began. Most of the Bible schools teachers or theologians make a clean sweep of the threefold Ministry of Christ. Nevertheless, it's so important to talk about that I ask you to pay attention. Therefore, in proportion as I explain it to you, little by little that will be understood. Let me deal now with the second part of Ministry of the suffering Messiah

G: The Mininistry of Christ upon the cross

The second part of the suffering Messiah lasted less than a half day for it was about the sixth hour and there was a darkness over all the earth until the ninth hour sixth hour when Jesus died: Luke 23:44. But before he gave up the ghost, on the very cross, Jesus fulfilled between the earth and the sky a triumphant Ministry of which we pay less attention. So I ask you to be patient in allowing me to explain to you how successful was the Ministry of Christ upon the cross. Let's begin. When Jesus went to start his Ministry upon the earth, he did that by forty days and forty nights of prayers, he began his Ministry between the earth and the sky by a prayer too: Father, forgive them for they not know what they do: Luke 23:34. When Jesus was on the cross, he was exercicizing his Ministry as a High Priest presenting to his father the last expiatory sacrifice for the entire world. I want just to make it clear for you because most of those who read and interpret the Bible, they think that Jesus was praying only for those who betrayed him or for the roman soldiers who have brutally beaten him. Absolutly not! That prayer, Jesus did it for those who betrayed him to be crucified, for those who dinied his messiahship and for all men from that generation to the next. Does that mean the prayer of the last expiatory sacrifice make every men holy to please God without surrendering themselves to him as sinners? Of course, Jesus asked forgiveness for all of men around the earth but each and every single of us has to come to Jesus to receive that forgiveness. The prayer of the last expiatory sacrifice that Jesus made on the cross is like a money account that a father has opened for his children. That money belongs to them; they have just to recognize that and go to the bank to claim it. Do you understand that? The bank account is already opened, full of money at the children disposal, but if some of them recognize that only and claim that money, now, they become possessors of what the father make accessible to them as heirs. Now, what's about those who don't recognize that their father opened a money account for them? Just because they have money in the bank account doesn't make them possessors. But, while they are starving in deep needy, the money is still at their disposal in the bank account. This is the same thing with regard to all of men on this planet. In the blood of Jesus, there is forgiveness for all of them, but they have to come to claim it. That means, through the the blood of his Son Jesus, God the father opened an account of forgiveness for whosoever comes to claim, they will be served. I want you to underline this word: <u>Whosoever</u>. To understand better what I'm telling you, you must read John 3:16, where you can encuenter the plan of salvation of God for every single one of us: For God so loved the world that gave his only begottenson in orther that whosoever believe in him shall not perish but have the everlasting life: John 3:16. The Bible is clear about that. All men can be saved but all men shall not be saved; and I let you discover the reason by yourself. On the cross, Jesus was presenting the last expiatory sacrifice for all the human race as a High Priest. Let me tell you more about it to understand better what I mean. In the Old Testament, when the High Priest offered in the temple of Jerusalem, once a year, the expiatory sacrifice for the forgiveness of people, he had to do it according to the levitical principles. Before the altar, the High Priest had to pray face upon the air, with opened arms and the joint-heels. Let us see Jesus on the cross now. How do you see him? In the same posture: Face upon the air, with opened arms and the joint-heels. This is why I tell you that when he repeteated in prayer Psalm 22:2, Jesus was presenting the last expiatory sacrifice for all the human race. The Ministry of Jesus between the earth and the sky was a far-reaching one in such manner that we can't make a clean sweep of it. Do you remember the thief hanging by his side on the cross? He was saved between the earth and the sky when he recognized the kingship of Jesus saying: Lord, remember me when thy comest into thy kingdom. And Jesus said unto him, verily, I say unto thee, today, shall thou be with me in paradise. Luke 23:42-43. In his far-reaching Ministry between the earth and the sky, Jesus pronounced his seven words hanging on the cross. Let me start explain to you, by taking the seven words of Christ and after that, we will go further.

H: <u>The seven words of Christ on the cross</u>

full Explanations

The first word of Christ on the cross:

Luc 23:34:   Father, forgive them for they know not what they do.

According to God will, nothing happened accidentally in the Ministry of Christ; I mean by that, God had planed everything from rhe beginning. Let me explain one by one, the main reason of the seven words of Christ pronounced on the cross. The mean reason of the first word of Christ on the cross, (Father, forgive them for they know not what they do) was to accomplish one levitical ordinance and two prophecies of Isaiah. Let me start by the levitical ordinance, according to the mosaic laws: Leviticus 4:20: And he shall do with the bullock as he did with the bullock for a sin offering , so shall he do with this, and the priest shall make an atonement for them, and it shall be forgiven them. This bulluck in the Old Testament, was the shadow of Christ who had to come to give his life in sacrifice for you and for me. So, when Jesus, the slain Lamb came, the shadow disappeared letting place to the reality to succede. So, on the cross, Jesus was given once for the forgiveness of sin of the entire world. By his bloody sacrifice, Jesus-Christ fulfilled once all the levitical ordinances obliged by the mosaic laws. In Matthew 5:17, think not that I am come to distroy the law, or the prophets, I am not come to destroy but, to fulfill. Let us see now, what Isiaiah said about the Messiah, eight hundreds years before he came. Isiaih 53:5: For, he was wounded for our transgression, he was bruised for our iniquities, the chastisement was upon him; and with his stripes, we are healed. Isiaiah 53:12: Therefore will I divide him a portion with the great, and he shall divide the spoil with

26

the strong; because he hath poured out his soul unto death: and he was numbered with the transgressors, and he bare the sin of many, and made intercession for the transgressors. So, I think that you have enough explanation at your disposal to understand what Jesus was talking about when he said in Matthew 5:17: Think not I am come to distroy the law, but I am come, not to distroy, but to fulfill. He came to fulfill the law, and he did. Once you get knowledge on the first word that Christ-Christ pronounced on the cross, let's go to the second one.

The second word of Christ on the cross:
Luke 23:43:   And Jesus said unto him: verily I say unto thee:
            Today, shall thou be with me in paradise.

The second word of Jesus on the cross, was a prediction made by him, on the cross, a short of time, before he died. Why do I say this word was a prediction? Let me explain that to you. It's just because after his resurrection and his ascension to heaven, some 62 years ago after that, Jesus appeared to John in the Patmos Island to repeat the the same word, the same promise to him, in Revelation 2:7, saying: He that hath a ear, let him hear what the spirit saith unto the churches. To him that overcometh will I give to eat of the tree of life, which is in the midst of the paradise of God. Of course, Revelation 2:7 is a remind of what Jesus said to the thief hanging by his side, in Luke 23:43: (Verily I said unto thee today thou shall be with me in paradise). Let me make that clear for you. To understand how Revelation 2:7 relate to Luke 23:43, we must underline that phrase from Luke 23:43: <u>Today thou shall be with me in paradise.</u> Now, let's us underline also from Revelation 2:7, the following phrase: <u>To him that overcometh will I give to eat of the tree of life which is in the midst of paradise of God.</u> Let me explain to you now, how these two passages relate to one an other: (Luke 23:43 and Revelation 2:7). In Luke 23:43, do you know why Jesus said to the thief: Today thou shall be with me <u>in paradise</u> instead of <u>in the Abraham's bosom?</u> Let the Bible answer to the Bible. I encourage you to read these two passages which relate to one an other: Ephesians 4:8-10 and I Peter 4:6. Let us start with Ephesians 4:8-10: Wherefore he saith. When he ascended up on High., he led captivity captive, and gave gifts unto men. Now that ascended, what is it but that he also descended first into the lower parts of the earth? He that descended is the same also that ascended up far above all heavens that he might fill all things. I Peter 4:6: For for this cause was the gospel preached also to them that are dead , that they might be judged according to men in the flesh, but live according to God in the spirit. It is for no reason that I submit these two passages to your interpretation. It is just because the answer is in both of them. Here is what I mean: Jesus didn't give the appointment to the thief hanging by his side in Abraham's bosom because he knew that when he will descend into the grave, he will empty the Abraham's bosom by moving from there, all the believers to paradise. That means, before the fulfillment of Ministry into the hell of Christ, the Abraham's bosom was the dwelling of the true believers. But, according to these two passages, the gospel was also preached to the captives in order to be judged according to God, at the doomsday. To be more accurate, let me put it this way: you who are reading this book, when you die, your soul will not be sojourned in Abraham bosom; she will be in paradise, waiting for the permission of the second Adam (Christ), to eat of the tree of life which is in the midst of the new Eden of God. Now, let us go to the <u>third word of Christ</u>.

*   *   *   *

=CHAPTER FOUR=

The third word of Christ on the cross:

John 19:27:   Woman, behold thy son! Then saith he to the
                  disciple: behold thy mother.

To understand the depth of what I am about to tell you, in regard of the third word of Christ, you get to know that the Bible, inspired by God, was written by the jewish people; it is from the jewish culture and, you have to remember also that Jesus was a Jew. The jewish people respect the Bible ancestral traditions from one generation to the next. One of the most respected one from the Bible is the <u>birthright</u>. According to the jewish ancestral traditions, when a child is a boy; when he was the first-born in his family; because of that, he got the supremacy over all the other children; he had a certain parenthood. According to the jewish traditions, the male who has the birthright, has also double in each part of the parental heritage. Above all, with his birthright, the first-born is the next responsible of the family after his father death. I mean, the first-born gets the family at his charge(his own) to be feeded, while the living mother profits of her dot. When the first-born is getting old or when he is dying out, he has to find out a worthy and reliable person to take over. It was exactly the case about Jesus, because, he was the first-born of his family. He got the birthright over his family after Joseph death. When you read carefully the theachings of Christ from the New Testament Bible, you can discover from him, not only a spiritual leader, a Messiah, but a very responsible man at a social perspective point of view. Because of the importance of the birthright, if the first-born has no male heir to give it, he gets the freedom to choose a reliable person to take over. It was the case, when Jesus said to the disciple <<woman, behold thy son! And he saith to the disciple: Behold thy mother.>> By his word, Jesus was exercising his birthright and his parenthood toward his motherly family before he died. It was like the last word of his last will about his birthright to be sure that the motherly family was in a reliable person hand. Therefore, the declaration of Jesus has nothing to see with any kind sort of marial cult.

* * * *

The fourth word of Christ on the cross:

Matthew 27:46   And about the nineth hour, Jesus cried with a loud voice, saying: Eli, Eli, lamasabac'thani? That is to say: My God, my God, why hast thou forsaken me?

On the fourth word of Christ, there is a fact where I ask you to Pay attention. What is the fact? I want you to underline the fact that the fourth word is finished by a question mark. Above all, the most tremendous thing was the fact that the father never answered to his Son question. Why the father left the question risponseless? Did the father bispise his Son as though he didn't understand what he meant? Did Jesus-Christ ask the question to be answered by the father? All these questions deserve some details but I'm gonna do a synopsis of them in order to give you a short answer. If I say <<yes>>, I have to explain why; if I say <<no>>, I have to explain. Which one is the best answer? Yes or no? The answer is <<no>>. Why? Let the Bible answer to the Bible. Let us see what Psalm 22:1-2 say about that: My God, my God, why hast thou forsaken me? Why art thou so far from helping me, and from the words of my roaring? O my God, I cry in the daytime, but thou hearest not; and in the night season, and am not silent. Do you understand the answer? It is not mine, it is from the Bible. I want you to understand that. This prophetic Psalm 22 was written by David, one thousand years before Christ where God fortold that event on the cross. What do I mean by that? When Jesus-Christ cried, asking that to the father, it was to fulfill that prophecy in Psalm 22:1-2. So, what happened, happened according to God will; that got to be. Because of that, the father was right to keep silent, for, he already knew that his Son had to ask that question without expecting a risponse. That is to that Jesus was not waiting for an answer from the father. If you don't understand the answer in the first time, read it again and again until you get it. So, let's move on to the fifth word.

* * * *

The fifth word of Christ on the cross:

John 19:28   After that, Jesus, knowing that all things are now accomplished, that the scripture might fulfilled, saith: I thirst.

The fulfillment of the sacrifice of calvary was prepared by God from the eternity, years before the foundation of the world. When Jesus was on the cross, one of the most strange event that happened to him,

Was to receive from the roman soldiers a bitter vinegar. What was the objective of that? Did the roman soldiers try to kill Jesus on the cross by poisoning him? What kind drink was that vinegar? Before I go further, let me go back to 29 and 30 verses of Jean 19:28, where we are told about a vessel full of vinagar, filled by the roman soldiers to put in Jesus mouth being on the cross. The verse 30 tells us that when Jesus therefore received the vinagar, he said: <<it is finished.>> And bowed his head, and gave up the ghost. Even by curiosity, it is very interesting to know a little about this kind vinagar used by the roman soldiers. Be ready to get insight of it. As you know, the roman empire was the only military Super-Power ruling the entire world at that era. So the roman army was everwhere around the world to occupy territories, even below of the Mediterranean Sea. So, Jerusalem was under the roman empire domination too. At that era, the roman empire had the political control over the jewish population and the Sandhedrin had the religious power. So the roman military power kept with hardness the jewish population under subjection. Because of that, the roman soldiers were the most detestable all over the country. When the roman soldiers envaded a territory, they became slaves of it, for the enemies tried very often of killing them to retake the position back. So, because of the hardness of a roman soldier task, he was more than a slave. In fact, living far from his family and his motherland, very tired after a day of hard labour, he became the easy prey of the gross fatigue. So, a roman soldier was always a died-tired one. Therefore, a solution got to be found to keep the soldiers on watch. It was the reason why, most of them were drug-addicts. So, to prevent themselves from sleeping while service, the roman soldiers brought with them a sort of drink called <<posca>>. The posca was a fermented wine. To keep the posca in good condition of conservation, it depends upon what kind of recipient the roman soldiers put it, for a sample careless could change the wine into vinagar. It is the reason why the Bible calls this drink <<vinagar>>for the roman soldiers didn't keep the posca in good condition of conservation. Above all, the posca was like an antiseptic, a pain-killer or an anesthesia for them. Very often, the roman soldiers mixed the posca with the opium to make drug. By this proceeding, the posca became bitter as gall. So, to prevent themselves from being sleepy, tired and painless, the roman soldiers had always a lot of this kind drink in their vessels, in their war-bags. Now, you are on the verge of understanding when the Bible talks, in John 19:28-30, about a vessel full of vinagar, and then they took a spunge to get some in Jesus mouth on the cross. It was that kind drink used by the roman soldiers to prevent Jesus from soffering. According to my point of view, it wasn't by wickness that they did so to Jesus; it was by pitty. Because, after being beaten up so wildly, a crown of thorns over his head, the body wounded covered of bloody stripes, the agony of Jesus was pitiful. Be that as it may, the Bible says that when Jesus had therefore received the vinagar, he refused to drink it. Do you know why he refused to drink it? It was just because he wanted to feel the soffering in its fullness; he wanted to take in his body all our pains to make sure that our salvation is defaultless and defectless. So, when Jesus said: <<it is finished>>, he meant it. This word was pronounced by Jesus on the cross, just to fulfill the prophecy of psalm 69:21: They gave also gall for my meat; and also in my thirst, they gave vinagar to drink. Let's move on the next word of Jesus on the cross.

*   *   *   *

The sixth word of Christ on the cross:

John 19:30:   When Jesus therefore had received the vinagar, he said: It is finished: and he bowed his head, and gave up the ghost.

Between the Sixth and the Fifth word of Christ on the cross, the explanation is interechangeable. It is the reason why, I shall give you a short insight, just to let you know that when Jesus said: <<it is finished>>, he meant by that the plan of man salvation is really achieved; <<It is finished>> is the penultimate word of Christ on the cross. But it has a deep meaning for each and every one of us who thinks that we can do something to help Christ to save us. No one can do something good to please God in order to deserve the salvation. <<It is finished>> is the epilogue of Jesus-Christ works accomplished on the cross, once for all mankind. One can be baptized; one can make forty days and forty nights of fastings like Jesus did; one can distribute all his fortune to nourish poors . . . that does'nt make God love neither more neither less because on the cross, what Jesus did is enough to save us. The only one thing we can do is to surrender our life to Jesus to get saved. The blood of Jesus is like a bottomless ocean neither border; it is open for any one, from generation to generation. The Bible says in Romans 5:20: Where sin abounds, grace abounds much more. That means, the generation of men of the past, the present and the future one will be ever able to exhaust the depth of the ocean of the precious blood of Christ. The penultimate word of Christ on the cross was like a warrior cry of victory after a battle. The victory of Christ is the victory of every believer, no matter what the tribulations: John 16:33: These things I have spoken unto you, that in me ye might have peace. In the world, ye shall have tribulation, but be of good cheer, I have overcome the world.

Every single thing that Christ had accomplished in his Ministry, he did it through his father.

If his Ministry of salvation was so successful it's just because he had his father Spirit in him.

Because he was on the verge of fulfilling his Ministry of man salvation, it is the reason of his last word to command his Spirit to whom it belongs, by accomplish the prophecy of Psalm 31:5 which says: Into thine hand I commit my spirit: thou hast redeemed me. O lord, God of truth.

The seventh word of Christ on the cross:
Luke 23:46:   Father, into thy hands, I command my Spirit, and having Said that, he gave up the ghost.

The seven words of Christ on the cross seem to be a synopsis of his far-reaching Mission on the earth; It's like someone who is coming up the end of his works and takes time to summit the epilogue for a brief insight of its contain. In fact, on the cross, Christ presented the last expiatory sacrifice on the altar (the cross), asking to his father to forgive all mankind; on the cross, he saved the thief hanging by his side, giving him the appointment to paradise; on the cross, Christ showed him at the same time as the sacrifice; as the High Priest; on the cross, he fulfilled all the Old Testament prophecies talking of him hundreds before his birth on the earth. An after that, he gave up the ghost. So, as you can see, the Ministry of Christ began on the earth after forty days and forty nights of fastings and finished on the cross by a short prayer: Father, into thy hands, I command my Spirit. By the seventh word, Christ accomplished the prophecy of Psalm 31:5: Into thine hand, I commit my spirit: thou hast redeemed me. O Lord, God of truth. We have already seen what Jesus-Christ fulfilled from the earth to the cross. These two phases of his Ministry were a far-reaching one. Now, we are coming up the last part of Christ Ministry that I call: The Ministry of Christ into the grave. This part of Christ Ministry is so important that we cannot take a sweep on it. So, it will be the last part that I have to deal with.

*   *   *   *

I: The Ministry of Christ into the grave.

Let me say that by way of informations: We are living in a universe made of mysteries where the intangible and the tangible seem to be in perfect connection but no one can tell where they start and where they end. One of the most part of the mysteries of the universe is about the human being. And the other hand, it about the hell and the paradise that we find in the Bible. We believe that both of them are real but we have trouble to indicate where exactly they are. But, the Bible doesn't let leave us completely without insight. In fact, about the hell, the Old Testament uses the word "Sheol", 63 times; "pit" 3 times and "Hell" 30 times. And the other hand, in the New Testament, to discribe the same reality, the Bible uses the grecs words Gehenna, Hades. Both of them mean "Hell" in English language. In the New Testament, "Hell" is translated 12 times by "Gehenna", in 12 verses; 10 times, by "Hades" 11 times, by "grave". It is good to get all these details but the most important thing is to determine where the grave is located. When we read the Bible, we have enough informations to know that the hell is in the center of the earth. In Psalm 63:9, we read: But those that seek my soul, to destroy it, shall go into the lower parts of the earth. In the Testament, Luke 16:19-31 let see clearly that the hell is in the center of the universe. Now, let me tell you something not to dread you but just because it is important to know. Here is it: When the believers and the pagans die, both of them go into the Sheol; but they don't descend into the same apartment. How do I explain that? Very sample. The Sheol is divided into two different compartments. One for the believers in God and the other one, for the believers in devil. The believers in God compartment calls "The Abraham's bosom" and the believers in devil compartment calls the "Hell". According to Luke 16:19-31, when Lazarus died, he went into the Abraham's bosom, whereas the rich man, went into the "Hell". That is a clear reality to let men realize that as human beings, when we get born on this planet, because of our nature, life is the first heritage we share together, the last one is death. But, all depends upon how each one of us spends his life and what kind path we have chosen. We are leaving in a fallen world where people get to choose between good and evil; between God and Satan for what we sowed is what we will reap soon or later; and we get to choose also between the paradise and the hell. Consequentltly, in order to get more details of the subject, let us start talking now of the Ministry of Christ into the Hell.

When dit Jesus-Christ start his Ministry into the hell? He started the last part of his Ministry, that very day of his burial. So, from that day to his resurrection from the deads, he has been in a far-reaching evangelical crusade in the midst of the sepulchral population for three days. What did Jesus-Christ accomplish so extraordinarly into the grave to consider his sojourn there as a far-reaching evangelical crusade during these three days? <u>The Ministry of Christ into the hell</u> began the very day of his burial in his tomb. Now, we are dealing with the hardest part, where the Bible says that Jesus-Christ went to preach the gospel to the dead people into the grave. For so many of those who don't understand, it is a big deal; it is something impossible to be done. But they forget what the Bible says in Luke 1:37: Nothing is impossible to God. I know more than anyone that once someone dies, his fate is set and then after somebody's decease, there is no salvation for him anymore. But what Christ did into the grave among the deads was something unic and exclusive, according to his authority and his grace. It was for the first and for the last time that happened. This is why Paul was told to say in Hebrew 9:27: And as it is appointed unto men once to die, but after this the judgment. This biblical passage is one of the arguments used by people to deny the fact that Jesus went to preach to the spirits into the hell. But they forget that word has been revealed to the author of Hebrew some thirty-five years after the resurrection of Christ. To deny the fact that Jesus went to preach the gospel to the dead people into the grave, some people used to say according to Matthew 22:32: I am the God of Abraham, and the God of Isaac, and the God of Jacob? God is not the God of the dead, but of the living. They just use these biblical verses out of context to deny a reality. If God is not the God of dead, but only the living, why there are the first and the second resurrections set up by God himself in the last day? Any way, the Bible is clear about that. Let me remind you what the Bible says about that. Let us read again I Peter 4:6: For for the cause the gospel preached also to them that are deads, that they might be judged according to the men in flesh, but live according to God in spirit. It was in God plan to be so. The gospel had to be preached first to them who died years before the coming of the Messiah. That event took place for the first and for the last time according to the exclusiveness of righteousness and the authority of God. So, believe it or not, that happened once at the a time. God made that expressly to let no one find an excuse to deny that fact that they had knowledge about the gospel of salvation in order to be judged according to the flesh at the doomsday. To give more evidence of that, the Bible says in Ephesians 4:8-10: Wherefore he saith, when he ascended up on High, he led captivity captive , and gave gifts unto men. Now that he ascended, what it is but that he also descended first into the lower part of the earth? He that descended is the same also that ascended up for above all heavens, that he might fill all things. I don't think you can find biblical passages clerarer that to explain what Jesus was doing during his far-reaching Ministry into the hell. It was like a three days crusade among the sepulchral population. Do you ever take time to think about that three days of crusade of Christ into the hell? It was a huge three days crusade not only for the deads around Jerusalem but all over the earth. I want you think about that. Before I finish, let me give you a synopsis of I Peter 4:6 and Ephesians 4:8-10: I know that is a moot case question to talk about. But let me explain that again, just to remind you. In the Old Testament, the Hebrew word for "Hell" is <<Sheol>>. The word <<Sheol>> is found 63 times in the Old Testament. Before the coming of the Messiah, before his death and his resurrection, from the Old to the Covernant, all the believers in God and the unbelievers, when they died, all of them went into the Sheol. But, let me tell you that they just took the same direction, not the same destination. What do I mean by that? According to Luke 16:19-31, the Sheol was divided into two different places, two compartments. One calls "the Abraham's bosom" and the other one calls "the Hell". "The Abraham's bosom" was the place set up by God himself for all the believers in him; the hell was and is for all the believers in Satan. According to Luke 16:22, when Lazarus died, he was carried by the angels into the Abraham's bosom. When the rich man died, he went into the hell. Some peolple think that the history of

Lazarus and the rich man is just a novel of science fiction. This is not. Quite the reverse, we should consider the history as the masterpiece of Christianity where Jesus-Christ lift up for the first time the curtain of the intangible world, to let the tangible creatures get insight of what is being processed in the outside of the universe. This is not a novel of a science fiction; this is exactly what happens when people die. Matter of fact, the rich man represents a category of men down here on the earth; Lazarus represents the other one. These two categories of men are always the same from generation to generation. But as we set up our bed, the way we lay down. The tangible world is the anteroom of the intangible one; the path you follow down here, leads you right to infinity; whether it be good or evil. So as I told you before, after the the <u>Ministry of Christ into the grave</u> for a three days crusade, the Abraham's bosom is empty; all of those believers were transferred directly into paradise. This is why Jesus did not say to the thief: Today, thy will be with me <u>in Abraham's bosom</u> <u>but in paradise</u>. It is the reason of this book. My objective is to let you know that Jesus-Christ had a threefold Ministry down here: The first part: His earthly Ministry; The second one: His Ministry <u>upon the cross</u> and the Third one: His Ministry <u>into</u> <u>the grave</u>. The other reason of this book is to let you know that until now, in the Sheol, the unbelievers of all generations are still soffering into the hell. But, after the second resurrection of deads, at the doomsday, they will be stand up before the Great Throne of God to be judgeds. After the last judgement, those unbelievers will not send again back into the grave; they will be cast out with Satan in the lake of fire forever: Matthew 25:41.

By the victory of Christ over Satan, he seized the keys of the death and the keys of the Sojourn of death; by the very triumph over the devil, Christ got back the lost Paradise to make it the dwelling place for His redeemed people. So, by way of informations, I want you to know that after the rapt of His Church to be in Heaven for the Weddings of the Lamb, for seven years, we will be come back on the earth with Christ for the Millenium that I consider as the honeymoon with His Spouse, the saved people. After the Millenium, Satan will be release for a short time, in order to provoke the last Battle of men history called the Harmaguedon. The fate of Satan and his followers is already set for the lake of fire. Now, according to the Bible, a new Heaven and a new Earth will be taking place for ever. So, the will of God will be done on the earth as it is in the heaven.

=EPILOGUE=

The threefold Ministry of Christ is written in four chapters, divided in titles and sub-titles. This presentation is a synopsis of a huge book that I have written first in French to be published, at the same time than the English Version. I invite you to read it with interst in order to discover in details, the messages and the blessings that the Lord puts at your disposal. When you are reading this book, I encourage you to check, one by one, all the biblical references to realize that the content of this work is not a make-up of my own ideas but something inspired by the Holy Spirit. To facilitate your task in reading in this book, here is the

=THE BIBLIOGRAPHIES=

- The Dr. Scofied Bible/Edition 1967
- The New interlineary greek /French Bible by Maurice Carrez, with Georges Metzger and Laurent Galy The Universal Alliance 5th Edition
- Commentaire biblique du chercheur/Nouveau Testament by John Walvoord. Roy. B. Zuck, based on the Segond version Bible 1979/Edition Geneve
- Willington's Guide Bible, by Dr. H. L. Willington/ Tyndale House Inc Weaton Illinois
- 7poems, 7 songs from the Seven Christ words on the cross Published in France 1994, recorded in 1994 à La Maison des Gens lettrés/France; Second publishing in the United States, 1999, By Wilson Douce Press, New-York.